SILLY JOKES FOR 8 YEAR OLDS

Which Mexican food does Thor love to eat?

Thor-tillas!

What did the rude bee say to the Queen bee?

Just buzz off!

How does the Easter bunny stay healthy?

He does plenty of eggs-cercise!

Why do gorillas need large nostrils?

To fit their large fingers!

What can you call a noodle that is fake?

An im-pasta!

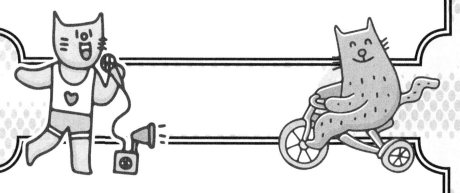

What food do most sprinters eat before they race?

Nothing. They fast!

What could you call an alligator wearing a vest?

An investi-gator!

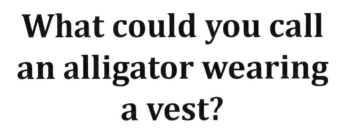

Why was the pony unable to sing in the choir?

Because he was a little horse!

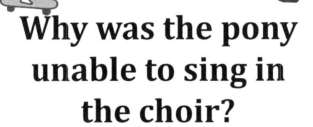

What did the magician say to make the rabbit disappear?

Hare today, gone tomorrow!

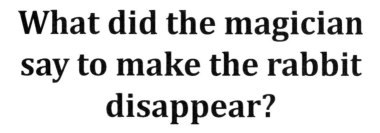

Knock, knock.
Who's there?
Hood.
Hood who?
Hood do you think you are?!

What do elephants use to stay cool?

Ear conditioning!

Why shouldn't you play hockey with pigs?

Because they just hog the puck.

How does a cat make a pizza?

They make it from scratch!

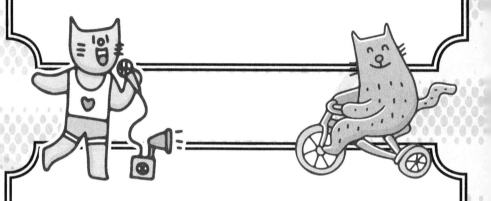

Which of Santa's reindeer always gets detention at school?

Rude-olf!

Which stories do rabbits love to read?

Stories that have hoppy endings!

What do you call a shellfish mixed with a rabbit?

The oyster bunny.

Why does Ant Man never have a wrinkled suit?

Because he always uses the Iron Man!

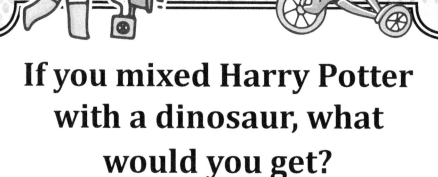

If you mixed Harry Potter with a dinosaur, what would you get?

A Dino-sorcerer!

Which bird gets out of breath a lot?

A puffin!

Which part of a fish weighs the most?

Its scales!

What made the student eat her homework?

Her teacher said it was a piece of cake!

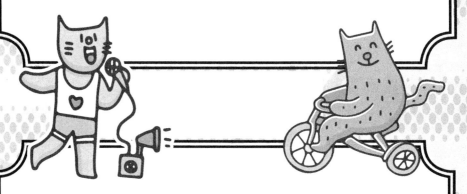

What do elves do when they get home from school?

Their gnome-work!

Knock, knock.
Who's there?
Cash.
Cash who?
No thank you, but I'll try a peanut if you have any!

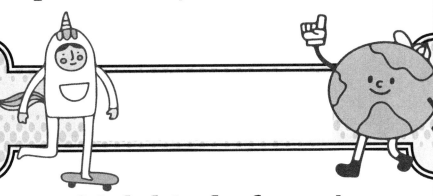

Which kind of movies do pandas love watching?

Old black and white movies!

Which movie do pirates love the most?

The Avengarrrrs!

What did mama cow say to her calf?

"It's pasture bedtime."

How is a piano different to a fish?

You can tune pianos but you cannot tuna fish!

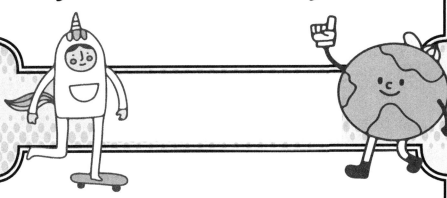

What do cats love to browse for new clothes?

The latest CAT-alogue!

Mr. Orange and Ms. Orange live inside the orange house;
Mr. Green and Ms. Green live inside the green house.
So who lives inside the white house?

The president, of course!

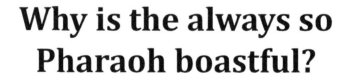

Why is the always so Pharaoh boastful?

Because he always Sphinx he's better than everyone!

Why do cats love sitting near to the computer?

They think they will be able to catch the mouse!

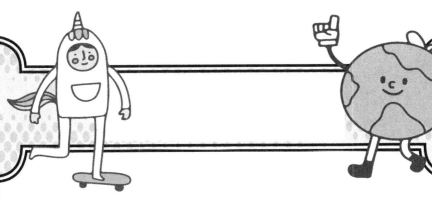

Why did the chicken run across the road?

It wanted to get away from KFC!

Why did the detectives investigate concert in the pond?

They knew something fishy was going on!

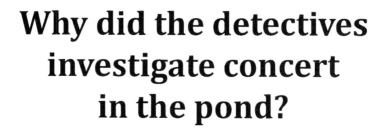

How should you help a pig when its injured?

Call the ham-bulance right away!

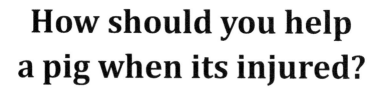

How did Pharaohs communicate with superheroes?

Using Hero-glyphics!

What happens when two giraffes collide?

You get a giraffic jam!

What is my computer friend's favorite bedtime snack?

Computer chip cookies and milk!

Which vegetarian dish do librarians love?

Peas and quiet!

What type of bees eat brains?

Zom-bees!

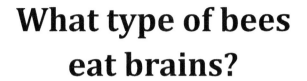

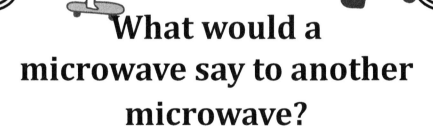

What would a microwave say to another microwave?

Is it me? Or is it getting hot in here?!

What type of tree can you fit in your hand?

A palm tree!

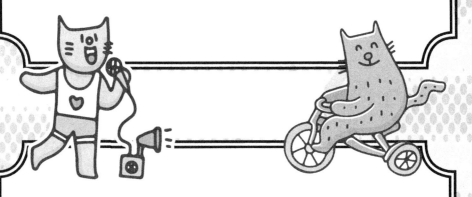

How can you raise an elephant baby?

Using a forklift!

Why did the snowman look in the box of carrots?

He was picking his nose!

Which card game did the ancient Egyptians love to play?

Gin Mummy!

What did the sunflower say when it told the bee a joke?

I was only pollen your leg!

Why are magicians always so good at solving riddles?

They know how to handle trick questions!

Why did the burglar need to have a shower?

He was trying to make a clean getaway!

Why do French people like to eat snails?

They dislike fast food!

How can a barber get to work early?

By using short-cuts!

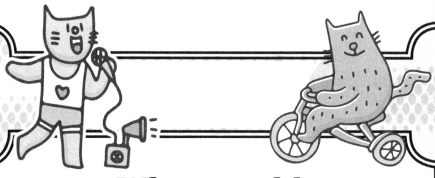

What would a llama say if it got told to leave the zoo?

Fine! Alpaca my bag!

What would a camel tell a hunter?

I think you need more camel-flage!

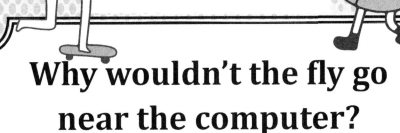

Why wouldn't the fly go near the computer?

He didn't want to get caught in the World Wide Web!

Where should you take a rabbit if their hair gets too long?

To your hare stylist!

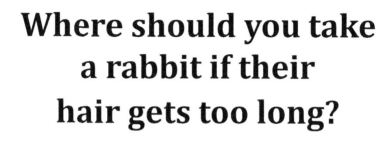

What would you say to your friend Pete if you couldn't hear what he said?

Can you re-Pete that please Pete?!

What would you call a polar bear in the sunny desert?

A solar bear!

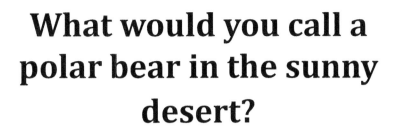

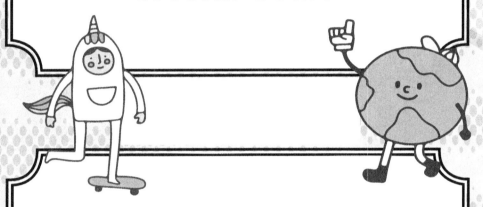

What makes fish so clever?

Because they live in schools!

Why do dentists need to help computers?

Because they usually have bluetooth!

Why did the horse eat with its mouth wide open?

It had awful s-table manners!

What could you call a chicken that counts its eggs?

A mathema-chicken!

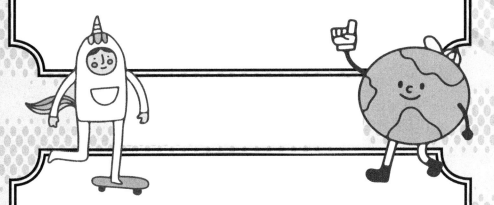

Which breed of dog would Dracula keep as a pet?

A blood hound!

Which holiday was the most important in ancient Egypt?

Mummy's Day!

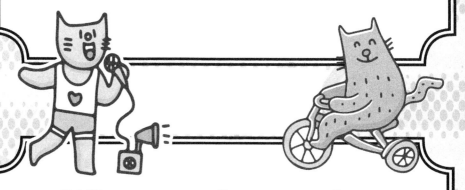

Why was the monkey tempted by the banana?

Because it was very appealing!

One muffin in the oven said "wow, it's hot in here!", what did the other one say?

"Ahhh! A talking muffin!"

How can you stop an astronaut's baby crying?

Just rocket gently!

Which type of year do frog's love?

A leap year!

If it took 8 builder 8 days to build a bridge, how many days should it take 5 workers to build the same bridge?

None - the bridge is already built!

How can you fix a tomota that's broken?

Use tomato paste!

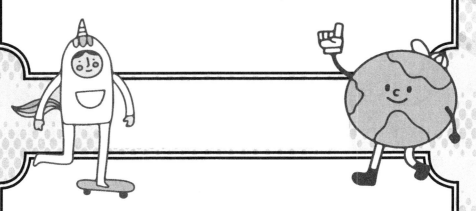

What do you call a duck that's very sarcastic?

A wise quacker!

Where do sheep love to go on vacation?

To the Baaaa-hamas!

Which musical instrument can you find in the bathroom?

A tuba toothpaste!

Why was Simba upset with Timon?

*Timon called him
a mere cat!*

Which letter of the alphabet do golfers love?

Tee!

Which school subject are snakes the best in?

Hisss-tory!

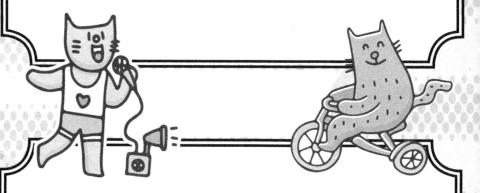

What do trains do at the Egyptian train yard gate?

They toot-and-come-in!

Why must fish only live in saltwater?

Because pepper would make them sneeze!

Knock, knock.
Who's there?
Utah.
Utah who?
U talking nonsense!

Why didn't the clam want to share her food?

She was too shellfish!

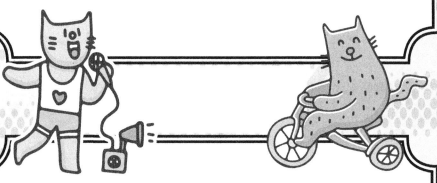

What did the calculator say when the other calculator needed help?

Don't worry, you can count on me!

Why did they ban the clock from the library?

Because it was tocking too much!

Why do dinosaurs not eat skunks?

Because they're ex-stink-t!

After many long years, the prisoner was released.
He ran around shouting, "I'm free! I'm free!"
Then a small boy walked up to him and said, "Yeah? Well I'm 4!"

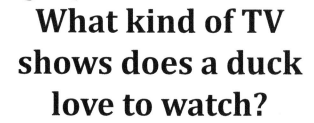

What kind of TV shows does a duck love to watch?

A: Duck-umentaries!

Why did the scientist love to wear denim?

He was an absolute jean-ius!

Why are snails the strongest insect?

Because they can carry their houses on their backs!

What should you do when you see a spaceman?

Park your car, man!

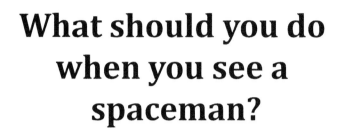

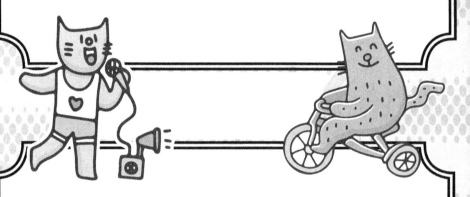

Where does a shark go on vacation?

Fin-land!

Which day are the most twins born on?

Twos-day!

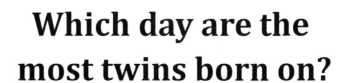

Why did the lions get hungry at the jungle party?

Nobody brought the tasty chimps and dip!

Who inspired Peppa Pig to love painting?

Pig-casso!

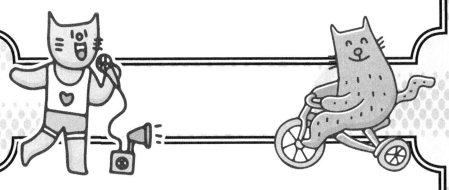

What stays in a corner but travels anywhere in the world?

A stamp!

How many dinosaurs can you fit inside an empty box?

Only one. After that, the box won't be empty!

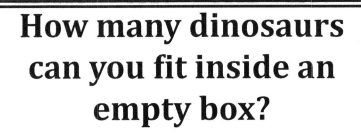

What gets washed up on tiny oceans?

Micro-waves!

What do you call a dinosaur sightseeing trip?

A Dino-Tour!

What did Scar say to Simba when was moving slowly?

Mufas-ter!

Why did the cow always get scared?

He was being a cow-ard!

What should you get when a lemon is hurt?

The lemon-aid box!

What sort of cat loves to go bowling?

An alley cat!

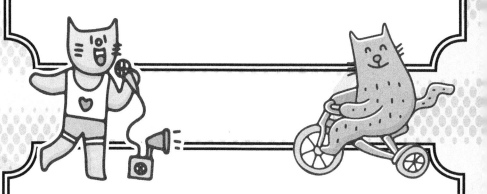

What kind of monkey can't keep a secret?

A blab-oon!

What is hairy, brown and wears shades?

A coconut on holiday!

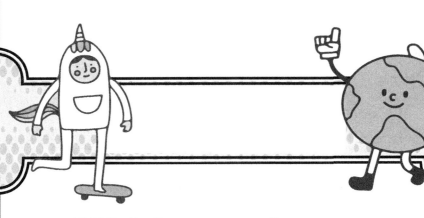

Which transformer can turn into a Gorilla?

Optimus Primate!

Which month makes the trees most worried about getting cut down?

Sep-timberrrrr!

What does the banana do if it sees a chimp?

It splits!

How can a cow blend in with its surroundings?

Using Ca-moo-flauge!

What would you get if you mix a rabbit with an insect?

Bugs bunny!

What would you get if a dinosaur walks through your raspberry patch?

Raspberry jam

What does a cow watch every evening?

The Evening Moos!

Why did the lamp float when it got dropped in the pond?

Because it was very light!

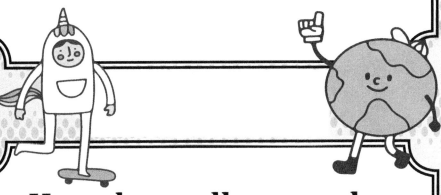

How does a llama wake up for college in the morning?

By setting their allama clocks!

What trick did the monkey use to go downstairs quickly?

He slid down the banana-ster!

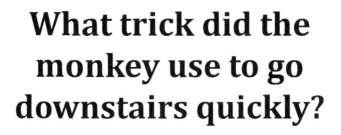

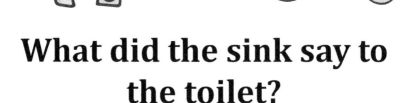

What did the sink say to the toilet?

I think you looked a bit flushed!

What do pig farmers give to each other on Valentine's Day?

HOGS & kisses!

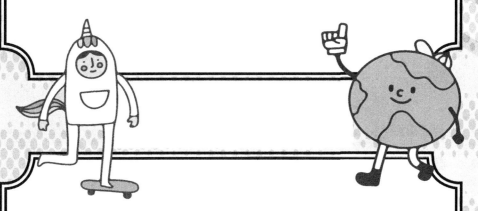

Do you want to hear a very long joke?

joooooooooooooooooooooke!

Which llama is the fastest?

A Llama-borghini!

How do you know if the moon has eaten too much?

When it's a full moon!

Why are porcupines the best at playing games?

They always have the most points!

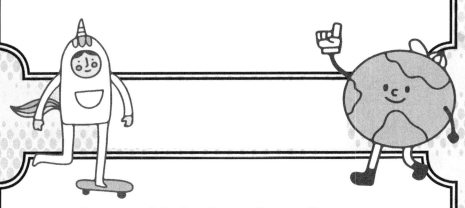

What did the herbs say when the spices had a problem?

Do you want us to dill with it?

Why did the policewoman visit the baseball game?

She heard that someone was stealing bases!

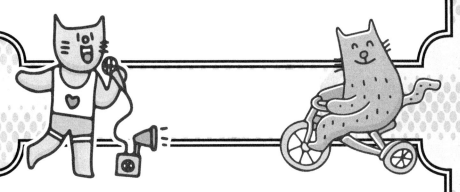

Who grants the fish their wishes?

The fairy cod-mother!

What would you call an elf who is greedy?

Very elfish!

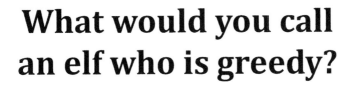

Which days of the week are the strongest?

Saturday and Sunday. The rest of them are weak days!

Why did the science teacher have smelly breath?

He forgot to do his experi-mints!

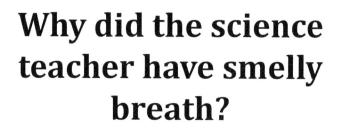

Why are spiders such good computer programmers?

Because they know all about the web!

What did the store owner say when he saw two pennies walk in?

That makes cents!

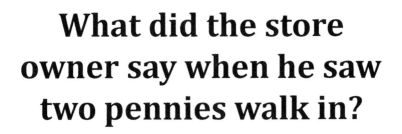

What happens if you cross a pig with a dinosaur?

You get Jurassic Pork!

Which part of Christmas do mummies like the most?

Present wrapping!

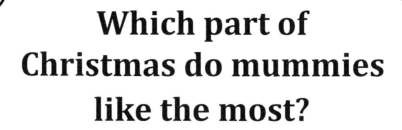

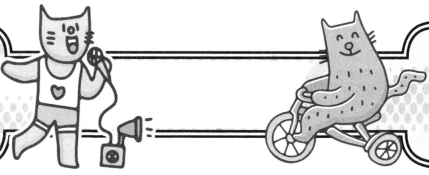

What made the book want to join the police?

It wanted to go undercover!

Why was the droid late for its maintenance cleaning?

Because it took an R2 detour!

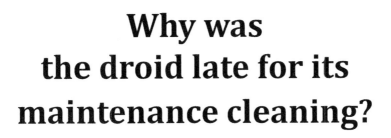

How do squids get to school?

They take an octobus!

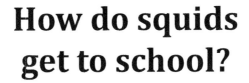

Which owl has the strongest force?

Owli-wan-kenobi!

Knock, knock.
Who's there?
Dishes.
Dishes who?
Dishes the police, open the door!

What would you get if you mix a crocodile with a computer?

A mega biter!

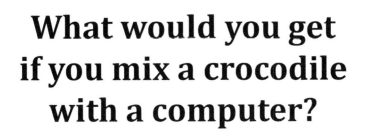

How can trees use computers?

They just need to log on!

Why is Simba so good at rowing canoes?

He has a huge r-oar!

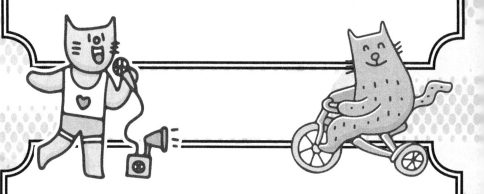

What kind of tree has lots of friends?

A Poplar tree!

What would you call a dinosaur that never gives up?

A Try-Try-Try-ceratops!

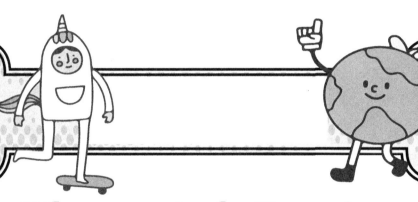

What music do Egyptian mummies listen to when they're bored?

Wrap music!

What would you call a bee that can't make its mind up?

A may-bee!

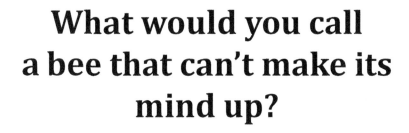

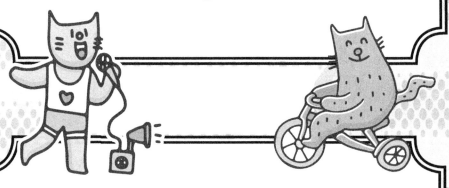

Which US city do eggs love to visit the most?

New Yolk!

What would you make when you cross a centipede and a parrot?

A walkie-talkie!

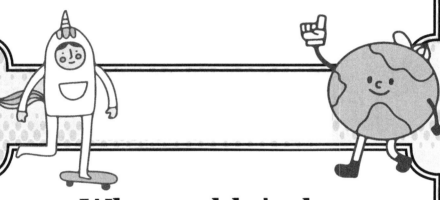

Why couldn't the hyenas cross the road?

They were too busy laughing!

Why can't leopards play hide and seek?

Because they are spotted all the time!

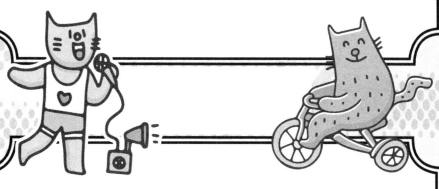

Which winter sport do maths teachers love?

Figure skating!

Why did the dragon walk across the road?

He was too chicken to fly!

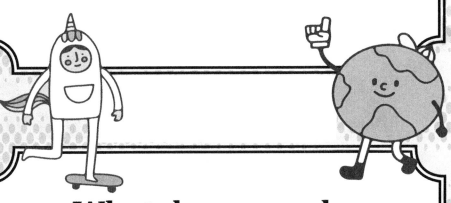

What do you make if you cross a cow and a camel?

Lumpy milk!

What would you call a cow lying down on the grass?

Ground beef!

Which baseball team do all lions love?

The Cubs!

Which part of a computer keyboard do astronauts love?

The space bar!

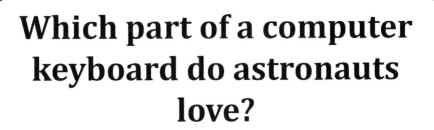

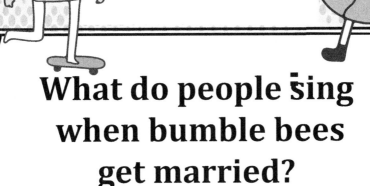

What do people sing when bumble bees get married?

Here hums the bride!